Just like a Star

Maddie Rose

BookLeaf Publishing

India | USA | UK

Presentation by *BookLeaf Publishing*

Web: www.bookleafpub.com

E-mail: info@bookleafpub.com

ISBN: 9789358319019

First edition 2024

DEDICATION

For Myself and the people similar.

To everyone who isn't good at living

and to My Mother.

PREFACE

As I said, I am not a poet. In fact, ever since I was a child I have hated poetry. But all I knew was that it had to rhyme which I couldn't stand. Now as I have grown up I've been very interested in philosophy and thinking and feeling harder than most. Along this journey I've come to really enjoy poetry as I found it freeing and enjoyable. Being able to albeit poorly write down these things in a meaningful and interesting way has in some way helped me. The majority of these come from my heart and soul though I must say one or two have come as short versions of books I'd like to write some day.

And Just Like A Star

And just like a star,
She shone brightly in the dark
And just like a star
She was adored by the people

But the people just stargazed
And just like a star
She faded away unknown.

Soul

More understanding we share
Than one bound by blood.
Together, we create soul.

Marcid

I can't walk
I can't decide
I can't talk
I can only reside
On the lone pearl
In my own head

I'm too worn
From the waves
I can barely feel in form
Within my caves

I'm withering.

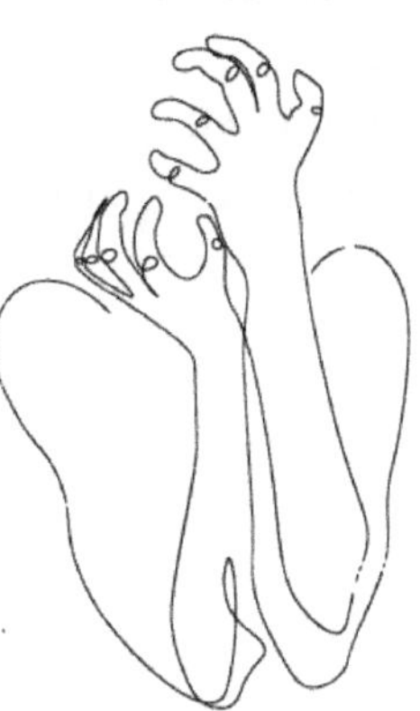

Saudade

My body
My matter
My soul
My being
It is all but dust
Tiny stars
All crushed
Reduced to saudade.

Fool

Cruelly mislead, I thought we bled together
But it seems, your name was Joachim and mine
was Cain.

Time

I cannot accept
The awareness of time

I yearn for a period
I never thought I would
I hated it back then
So why do I want it again so badly?

I hate the present
But I know
I'll yearn for it again
when a new present comes
Wishing I could've done something more
Than loathe the days counting by.

Naïveté

I thought we could understand
But this desire
Was all but a grand
Blunder by a crier.

Oh how naïve
this little star believed
Things would become
A little less numb.

Beauty & Tragedy

Born with innate beauty
Born with innate tragedy
The women braid each other's hair,
The women help each other dress
The women wail with one another
The women understand
The women sleep.

The women's love is theirs alone.

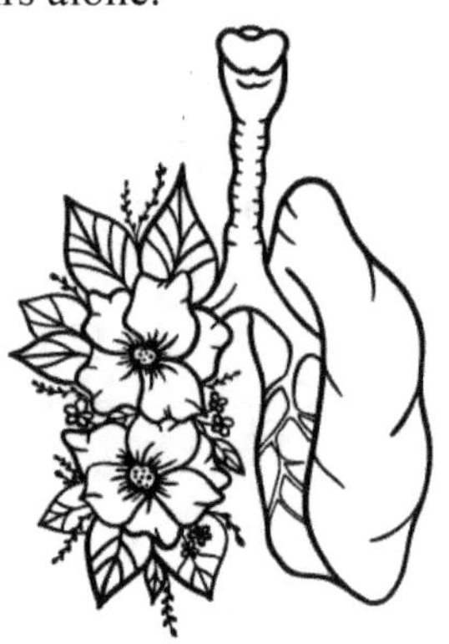

Little Lake

Looking into a puddle
I see a stranger
Feeling the rain on my skin
I can sense it's decay
Walking into the water
I cannot turn back
Don't look back
Don't give in to the urges
Doesn't your heart ache a little?
Let your eyes pour
Become soft
Remember to swim.

Nameless Pierrot

The nameless Pierrot dances for the world
But nobody knows why
What does the nameless Pierrot desire so badly?
He dances because there is nothing to do but
dance
It is all he has wanted for
It is all he needs.

Maybe this way
The nameless Pierrot
Will be nameless no longer
And will be remembered
As a someone instead.

Stuck

In the dead of night
I feel the weight
The skin I wear
Is a jail hard to bear
Eternally confined
My soul longs to be once again entwined
Among the stars dancing above,
To feel limits I am yet to know of.

Painting

I cry I bleed I deform I fail I fight
But that's what makes art so beautiful right?
As long as sorrow runs through
My whole will hold value.

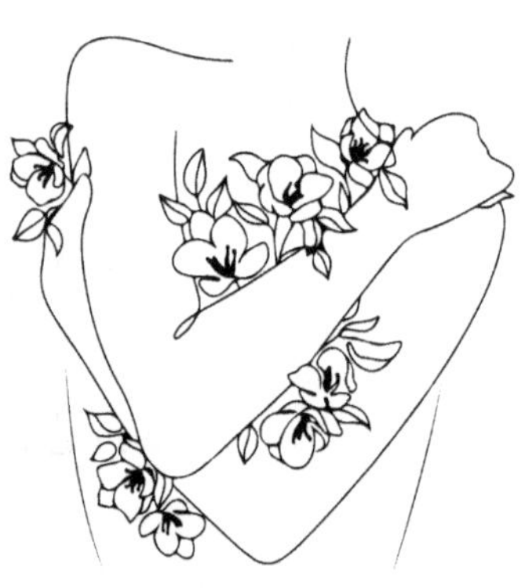

Content

No need for peace
Nobody understands and it hurts more to think
you might
No need for pity
I've stayed subsist for various nights
No need for you
pretending you're my releasing light.

Glass Doll

Smashing glass dolls
I feel as though I'm forgetting
A child regretting
The life they've let fall.

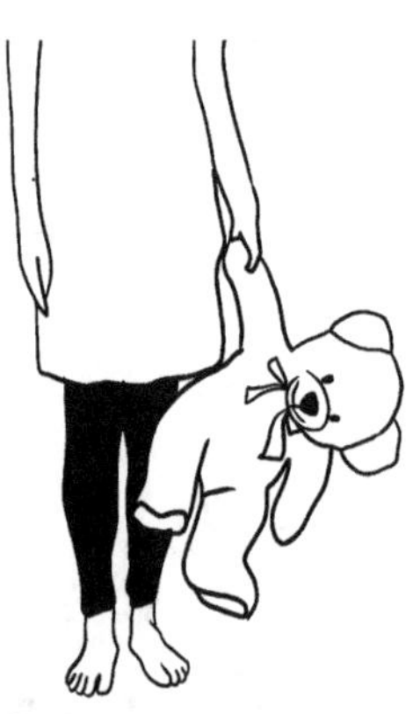

Wanderer

Disconnected from humanity
I wander along aimlessly
Wondering, when will I
Return home to the stars?

Desire to Dream

I cannot contain the star of creation
Yet I don't know how to let this star free.
Trapped in my own body,
Into little stars, it will explode
Just fragments of what once could've been
Left behind, yearning for Perseus
Missing the main piece.

Hands of Time

Time is getting younger
And I am getting older.
Nobody told me
The hourglass had been flipped,
The clock betrayed me.

The world only desires youth
But when it is my turn
I am not young enough.

I can feel myself becoming lesser and lesser,
dusting away
As the seconds I am lost with
Tick and tock away
Gone to the past so fast.

Only when it is too late
Do I realise
What I could've done.

Judas

Oh, Great lord
Would you love me dear,
If I was an experiment
Of all the world's turmoils
If I took the bribe of 30 silver
If I am not everything
I was meant to be.

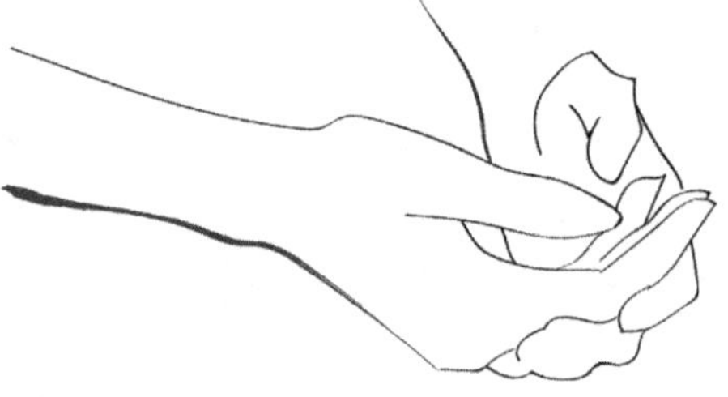

Home

Who plays the role of mother?
Who plays the role of father?
Who plays the role of sister?
And who plays the role of brother?
Where is your home?
Who made your home?
What is home?

me?

Faces disappear behind the show
Voices fade into the echo
I become a masquerade

In a world I fail to know
Leaving things I wish to not forego
My face is being massacred

Bittersweet

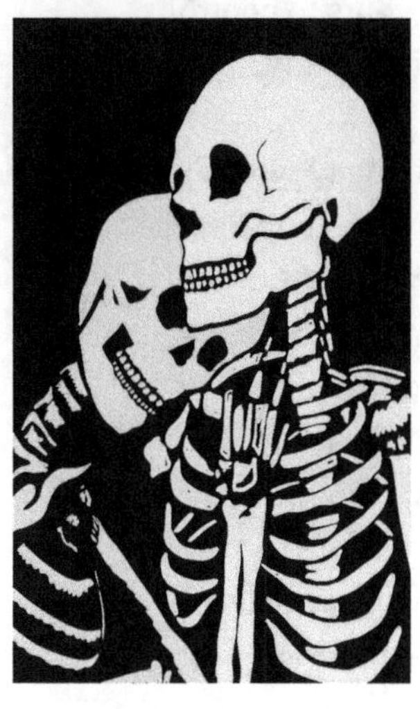

Enjoying is a hard thing to do
When all you want is something you can't have
But to find the beauty in this
Is a good feeling to live alongside
Find the beauty in anything
And you'll live a lovelier life.

The people we love
Will come and go
But even if they aren't out there anymore
They will still be
Existing, stuck in a place of the past.

The life you didn't have
Is the life you can live now
Your life is yours to control
Truly hold it strongly.

There are so many words to be said
But so very little time or space
Fleeting feelings
Won't forever be lost
Just to one day be found.

Enjoy every second you have
Even when you are sad
Make sure you use that well
Don't waste your time
You can't afford it

Happiness always feels so bittersweet